You Can Be Anything You Want To Be

This book is dedicated to my father, Robert Hindoveh Sam-Kpakra, who instilled great confidence in me and taught me to dream, to care and to love.

Forever in my heart, I miss you daddy.

ISBN 978-1-0880-9057-2
Odessa Katumu Sam-Kpakra

You Can Be Anything You Want To Be

Odessa Katumu
Sam-Kpakra

illustrated by Penny Weber

This is Katumu and her family. She grew up in a city called Bo in Sierra Leone, West Africa.

When she was a little girl, Katumu's favorite thing to do was to spend time with her father.

He loved to carry her, teach her to ride her bike
and encourage her to dream big dreams.

One day, Katumu and her daddy went for an evening drive. Katumu saw workers fixing the road and noticed a woman in a construction jacket.

"WOW!", she exclaimed, "Can I do that when I grow up?"

"Yes, my child, you can be anything you want to be. As long as you believe it in your heart", her father responded.

And so it was with Daddy.
Inspiring his little girl
to always dream and
never be afraid to try new things.

"Always find ways to change
your community for the better.
Remember, change resides in you,"
he would always tell her.

When Katumu was 15 years old, she left Sierra Leone to
continue her schooling in America.

As she said goodbye to her family,
her father cried and cried.
Katumu only smiled and laughed.
She was too excited to cry.

She arrived in America, and ran straight into the arms of her maternal grandmother and aunt who were waiting patiently for her at the airport.

The excitement continued for Katumu at her grandmother's house. Her grandmother had prepared a huge feast to celebrate her arrival.

That night, as Katumu lay in her bed, she thought
of her family in Africa.
She finally realized she had never been away from her parents
this long and for the first time, she wept and wept as she
longed for them.

Soon Katumu was in high school and started making friends

She sang in the choir, joined the glee club and helped out at school whenever she could.

After two years in high school, Katumu graduated.

She was now going to college.
She kept thinking back to the conversation she had with
her daddy years ago:

Katumu enrolled in college in pursuit of a degree.
But shortly after starting, she received
a telephone call from her uncle.

He had some very sad news to tell her.

Her wonderful daddy had passed away.

She was so very sad.
But she kept thinking
of the conversation
they had when she was seven.

"That's it!" she said to herself,
"I'll make him proud.
I'll become a Soldier and
serve my community."

So Katumu joined the Army, to fulfill her dream of
service and make her daddy proud.

After all, it was his words that had always and
would always serve as a drumbeat in her head,
and in her mind and soul.

Hearkening her to never forget –

"You can be anything
you want to be".